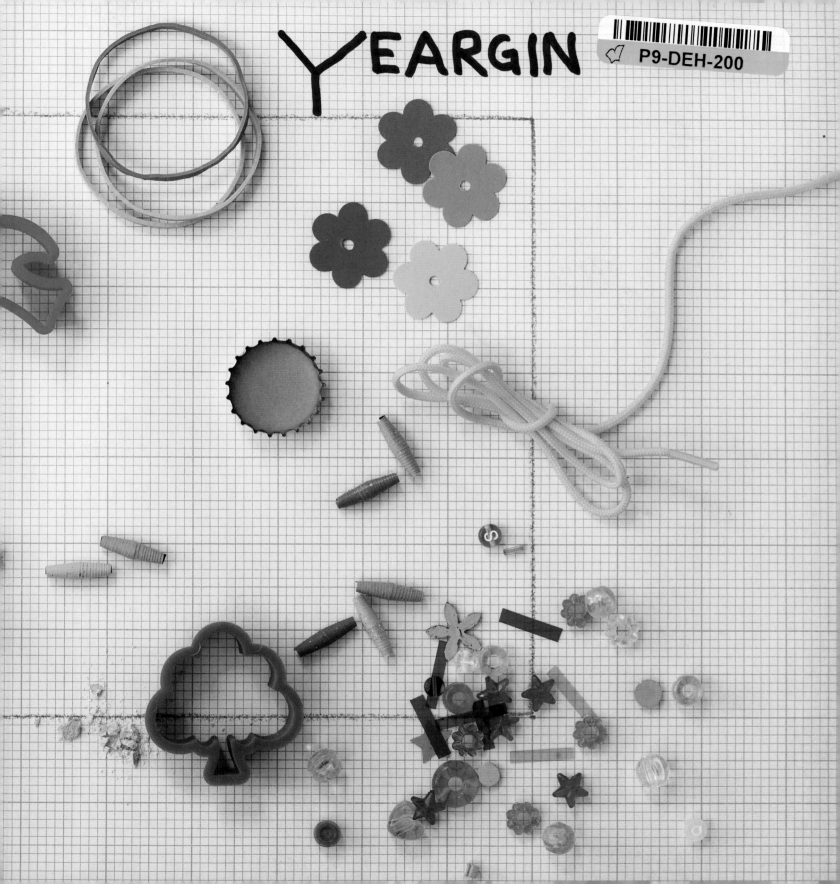

YEARGIN

eco-friendly crafting
with kids

eco-friendly crafting
with kids

35 step-by-step projects for preschool kids and adults to create together

by kate lilley of MINIECO

with photography by **carolyn barber**

RYLAND
PETERS
& SMALL

LONDON NEW YORK

Senior Designer Sonya Nathoo
Editors Annabel Morgan and Miriam Catley
Head of Production Patricia Harrington
Art Director Leslie Harrington
Editorial Director Julia Charles

Stylist Liz Belton

First published in 2012
by **Ryland Peters & Small**
20–21 Jockey's Fields
London WC1R 4BW
and 519 Broadway, 5th Floor
New York, NY 10012

www.rylandpeters.com

10 9 8 7 6 5 4 3 2 1

Text © Ryland Peters & Small 2012

Design and commissioned photographs
© Ryland Peters & Small 2012

ISBN 978 1 84975 204 6

A catalogue record for this book is
available from the British Library.

US Library of Congress cataloging-in-
publication data has been applied for.

Printed in China

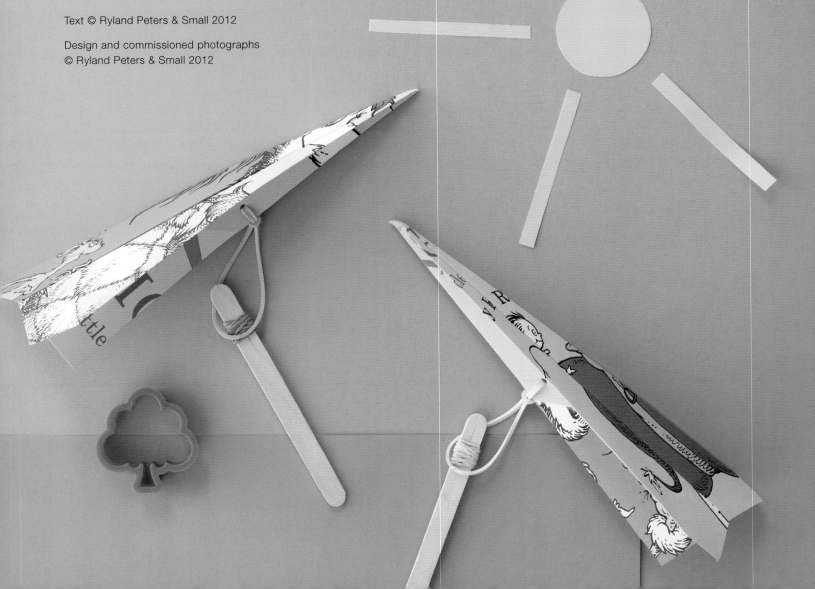

contents

introduction

As a new parent I was always told not to buy my sons expensive toys because, at the end of the day, they would always end up playing with the box. I smiled and nodded at the time (as you do!), but now my sons are four and three I can put my hand on my heart and say it's absolutely true!

Boxes, and other such household junk, have become treasured possessions in our house. My four year old is currently obsessed with cash registers and it is amazing to see him turn a cardboard box into a complex machine using little more than his imagination. Using household objects for crafting makes so much sense. It's cheap, kind to the environment and encourages kids to use what's around them for creative play.

Kids will need help and supervision for all of the projects in this book. To what degree depends on the child's age and ability. Needless to say, all steps involving sharp scissors, craft knives or ovens should be carried out by a grown-up and please remember that small objects, such as marbles, may be a choking hazard. Some of the projects in the book are also a bit messy, so make sure you gather all your supplies beforehand and have a washing-up bowl on hand for a speedy clean-up afterwards. Please don't be put off doing the messy projects, though, because they are the most fun and your kids will love you for it!

My sons, Seth and Tom, have road-tested all of the projects in this book. We've had a blast along the way. I hope you do too. Happy crafting!

homemade materials

Playdough

Making playdough is a science experiment, cooking lesson and craft project all rolled into one. We spend hours playing with it in our house, and there is always a lot of excitement in the air each time we whip up a fresh batch!

materials

- ½ cup of flour
- ½ cup of water
- ¼ cup of salt
- ½ tbsp cream of tartare
- 1 tbsp cooking oil

how-to

1 Get your helper to put all the ingredients in a pan and give it a good old stir. You can add some natural dyes to the basic recipe to make coloured dough (see page 13).

2 This step is for grown-ups only! Put the pan on a medium-low heat and continue stirring. Pretty soon it will start to look like something from a science fiction film and will stick to the pan – rest assured it will come good in the end! Once it forms a ball, turn the heat off and scrape the playdough onto a floured worktop.

3 Allow the dough to cool, then knead it for a few minutes until smooth.

4 Soak your pan in warm water for five minutes. After a quick wipe round with a cloth it will be as good as new!

hints and tips

- Needless to say, this recipe is for a non-edible playdough!
- Remember not to let your little one/s anywhere near hot or boiling water.
- Natural dyes can stain, so it's best to wear an apron when preparing them. I've never had a problem with playdough staining hands or clothes once it is made.

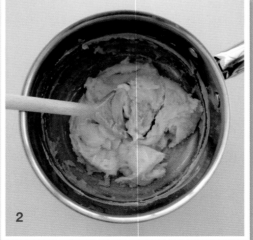

turmeric

raspberry

tree bark

beetroot/beets

cocoa

red cabbage

natural dyes for homemade playdough

Using natural plant dyes to tint your playdough is lots of fun and a lovely way to teach kids that some of the most beautiful dyes can be found in your own back yard.

turmeric

Stir 1 teaspoon of turmeric powder into the dry playdough ingredients, then follow the basic playdough recipe. To make the colour more intense, knead some more turmeric into the playdough once complete.

raspberries and blueberries

Put a big handful of your chosen berries in a pan with a cup of water. Bring the mixture to the boil then gently simmer on the stove for about five minutes. Once the liquid has cooled, pass it through a sieve, then follow the basic playdough recipe using half a cup of your natural berry dye to replace the water.

tree bark

Don't take bark directly from the tree – if you hunt around, you will find plenty on the ground. Put a big handful of bark in a pan with 1½ cups of water. Bring to the boil then gently simmer for 20 minutes, until the liquid has reduced to about a third. Once the liquid has cooled, pass it through a sieve, then follow the basic playdough recipe using half a cup of the tree bark dye to replace the water.

beetroot/beets

Chop up one medium-sized beetroot and put in a pan with a cup of water. Bring to the boil then gently simmer for a minute. Once the liquid has cooled, pass it through a sieve, then follow the basic recipe using half a cup of the beetroot dye to replace the water.

cocoa

Stir 1 teaspoon of cocoa powder into the dry playdough ingredients, then follow the basic recipe. To make the colour more intense, knead some more cocoa into the playdough once complete.

red cabbage

Chop up a handful of red cabbage and put in a pan with a cup of water. Bring to the boil then gently simmer for a few minutes. Once the liquid has cooled, pass through a sieve, then follow the basic recipe using half a cup of coloured liquid to replace the water. Red cabbage produces a blue dye, but it turns bright pink when added to the playdough mix!

eco info

This craft uses readily available materials with no toxic chemicals!

watercolour paints

I was amazed to find out you can make your own paints and, luckily, my kids think it's amazing too. It's also a two-fold activity, which means double the fun!

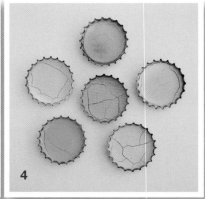

how-to

1 Get your little helper to mix the bicarbonate of soda, cornflour, vinegar and glucose syrup in a bowl. Keep stirring until the mixture stops fizzing.

2 Pour the mixture into small containers to a depth of about 1cm/½in.

3 Add 5 drops of food colouring to each container and stir with a toothpick. If you want a stronger colour, add a few more drops and continue to stir.

4 Pop your paints on a sunny windowsill to dry. It usually takes 1–2 days, depending on the weather.

5 Once your paints have dried out, give your little one some paper, a brush and a pot of water and let the painting commence!

hints and tips

You can make your own liquid glucose by adding ¼ cup of sugar to ⅛ cup of water in saucepan. Heat until the liquid begins to boil and all of the sugar has dissolved. Allow to cool before use.

eco info

This is a great way to re-use any old bottle tops and lids.

materials

- 3 tbsp bicarbonate of soda/baking soda
- 3 tbsp cornflour/cornstarch
- 3 tbsp white vinegar
- 2 tsp liquid glucose syrup
- Bowl
- Containers for paints (e.g., old bottle tops or ice-cube trays)
- Food colouring
- Toothpicks

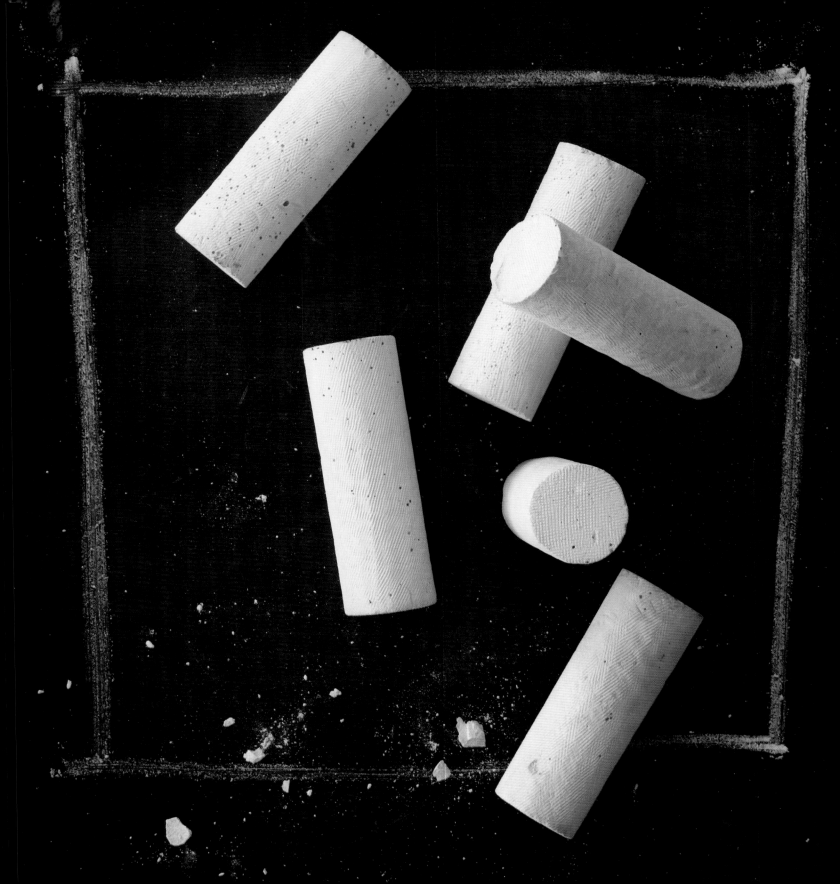

homemade chalk

Making your own chalk is really easy and lots of fun, and the end result provides you with a brilliant excuse to get outside and be creative – hurray!

how-to

1 Tape up one end of each cardboard tube with masking tape making sure that it is sealed.

2 Line the inside of the tube with a piece of greaseproof paper. Stand each tube, taped side down, on a level surface. Make sure you stand them on a piece of kitchen paper in case you get any leaks.

3 Pour the water into a plastic container then sprinkle the plaster of Paris on top (generally it's a 1:1 ratio, but check the instructions on the packet).

materials

- Toilet rolls/cardboard tubes
- Masking tape
- Greaseproof/wax paper
- Scissors
- Old plastic container
- 1 cup of water
- 1 cup of plaster of Paris
- 1 tbsp powdered tempera paint
- Stick (for stirring)

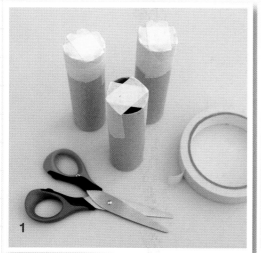

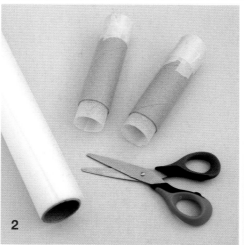

4 Add one heaped teaspoon of powdered paint to the mixture and give it a really good stir. If you want a deeper colour, add more paint.

5 Pour the mixture in to the tube and tap lightly to get rid of any air bubbles.

6 When the plaster has set you can remove the cardboard tube and greaseproof paper. You will need to allow the chalk to dry fully for a few days before using.

hints and tips

• If you feel your tube is too chunky, then cut it along the length, overlap the edges and tape them in place to reduce the diameter.
• Tin or silicon muffin pans also make great moulds and don't need lining with paper.
• Once you have made your chalk, go outside and play all manner of games. You don't even need to clean up – just wait for the next shower of rain to wash it away.

• Take turns to lie down on the ground and draw each other's outline. Add hair, face and clothes. If you are feeling adventurous, turn it into a biology lesson and draw some internal organs!
• Draw lots of roads and buildings then crack open the tub of cars and take them for a drive.
• Play beanbag toss. Draw lots of shapes on the ground with different numbers in. Take turns to throw the beanbags in and see who can score the most points.
• Play noughts and crosses/tic-tac-toe.

eco info
This project is a good way to re-use old toilet rolls.

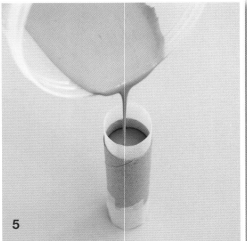

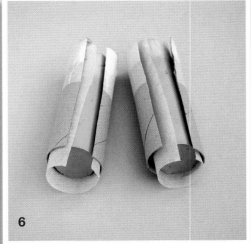

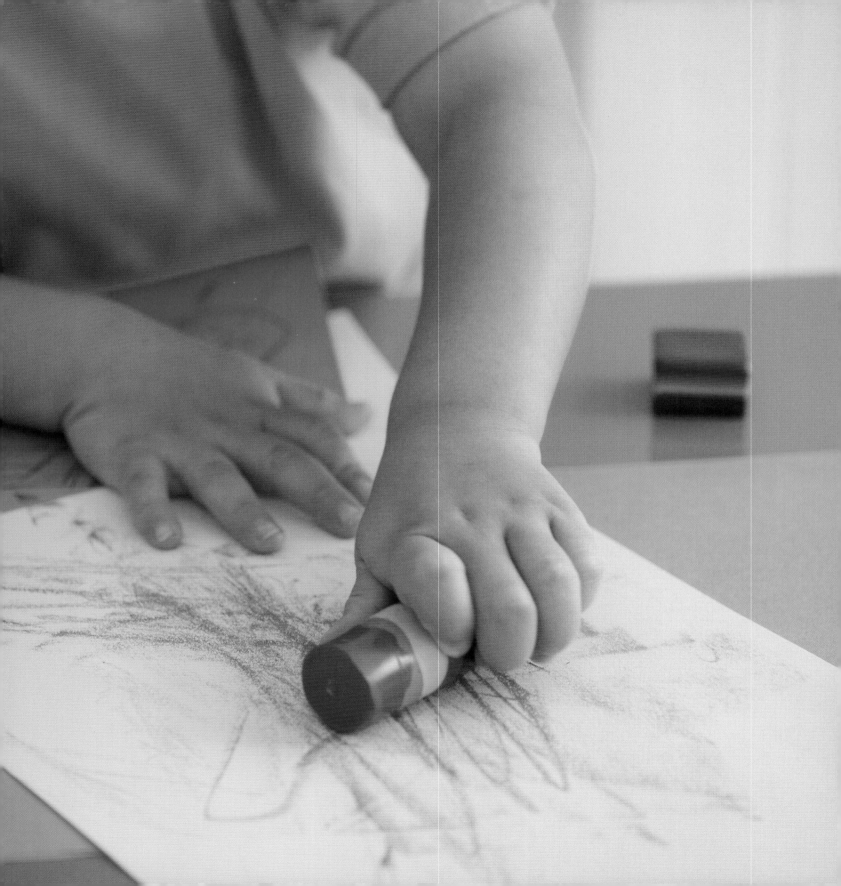

recycled rainbow crayons

This is a great way of breathing new life into all those broken (or half-eaten!) crayons. The result: beautiful, chunky rainbow crayons that are easy to hold and difficult to break – brilliant!

how-to

1 Ask your little one to snap all their old crayons into small pieces. Once this is done, sort the pieces into different coloured piles.

2 This step is for grown-ups only! Pour 5cm/2in water into a saucepan and bring to the boil. Reduce the heat to a gentle simmer. Put each pile of broken crayons into an empty, clean tin can and place the cans in the pan. Wait for the crayons to melt. You can use a stick to stir the crayon mixture, but don't forget to wear an oven mitt because the can will get hot!

3 Carefully pour the first can of melted crayons into several moulds, making sure you pour roughly the same amount into each mould. Pop the containers in the freezer for at least 5 minutes to set.

4 Once set, pour the next colour on top of the first. Repeat the process for each colour until you have used up all of your melted crayons.

5 Once the colours have set, tap the mould on your countertop to release the multi-coloured crayon.

hints and tips

If you are short on time, make muffin pan crayons instead. Simply break crayons into small pieces, pop into a muffin pan, and put into the oven on a low heat. As soon as the crayons have melted, remove them from the oven and leave them to set.

1

2

3

4

music

cardboard box guitar

You can make a pretty cool guitar from a simple cardboard box. I'd be lying if I said it was capable of knocking out Purple Haze, but Twinkle Twinkle Little Star is well within reach!

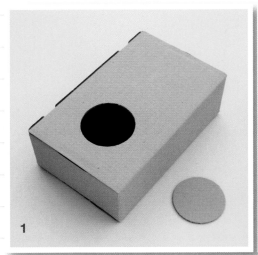 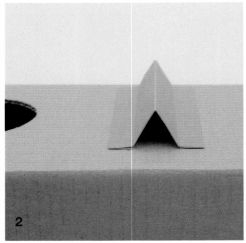 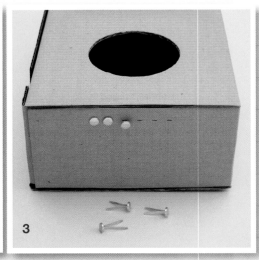

how-to

1 Take the cardboard box and tape the openings shut. Using a craft knife or scissors (grown-ups only!), cut out an 8cm/ 3¼in hole two thirds of the way down the face.

2 To make the raised bridge, take a piece of card measuring 12 x 6cm/5 x 2½in and score three horizontal lines along the length with a ruler and pencil. Fold the card as shown, and stick it to the box using the double-sided tape.

3 Push six paper fasteners in each end of your box, centred about 1cm/½in below the top edge. They need to be spaced about 1cm/½in apart.

4 Cut your rubber bands, then wrap one end around the first paper fastener. Pull the band to the paper fastener at the opposite end and wrap around again. Repeat with the remaining rubber bands.

5 To make the neck, take a piece of card measuring 20 x 35cm/8 x 13¾in. Score three lines along the length, 5.5cm/2¼in apart. Fold the card to form a triangular prism and secure the overlapping edge with sticky tape.

6 Using a craft knife or scissors (grown-ups only!), cut out a triangle with sides measuring 5cm/2in from the top of the body. Slot in the guitar neck. Once your guitar is complete, let your little one decorate it using felt-tip pens/markers or crayons.

hints and tips

• The tighter your rubber bands the clearer and higher the sound. It's essential to use a fairly strong box as otherwise it may collapse under the tension.

• Ask questions about how the sound changes when the the tension in the rubber bands is increased/decreased. Your little helper will notice that tighter rubber bands produce higher pitched sounds and looser rubber bands produce lower pitched sounds.

• If you are running short on time you can make a super-quick guitar by stretching some rubber bands across an open cake or cookie tin (square tins work best).

• Make sure there is enough space between the rubber bands so that they don't touch.

eco info

This project makes good use of unwanted cardboard boxes.

materials

• Sturdy cardboard boxes
• Sticky tape
• Craft knife/scissors
• Thick card or cardboard
• Ruler • Pencil
• Double-sided tape
• 12 paper fasteners
• 6 rubber bands
• Felt-tip pens/markers or crayons

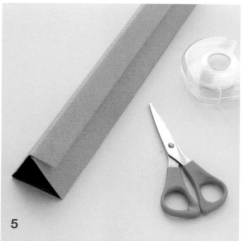

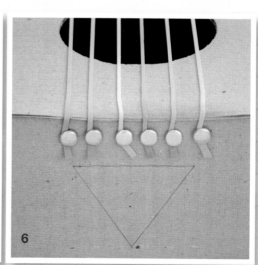

all-in-one bongo, shaker & guiro

This homemade instrument is a bongo, rice shaker & güiro all rolled into one. The best thing about it is that it's a doddle to make! Use chopsticks to bang on the drum or scrape down the sides of the güiro.

how-to

1 Scoop a small handful of uncooked rice or lentils into a clean can. Make sure the cans have smooth edges (most can openers today tend to leave a smooth edge on the tin). Coffee or infant milk formula tins also provide a great alternative to tin cans.

2 Cut the neck off the balloon. You may need to use sharp scissors, in which case this is a job for a grown-up.

3 Stretch the balloon tightly over the end of the tin. For extra durability use two balloons.

4 Secure the balloon/s in place with a rubber band. You're now ready to shake, rattle and roll!

eco info

This craft uses household and recycled materials.

materials
- Empty, clean tin cans
- Uncooked rice or lentils
- Balloons
- Scissors
- Rubber bands

ankle bells

Jingly-jangly ankle bells = lots of dancing fun. They also look amazing and make wonderful handmade presents for your children's friends and dance partners!

how-to

1 Cut two lengths of colourful wool/yarn, each one measuring approximately 1.2m/48in. Fold the wool in half.

2 Knot the folded ends of the wool together to form a small loop.

3 Pin the wool, by the loop, to a scrap piece of cardboard or polystyrene. Now the wool is secured you are ready to start tying knots in the four strands of wool.

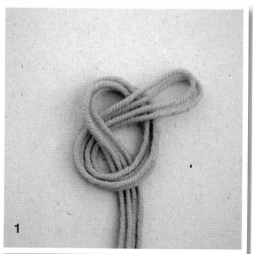

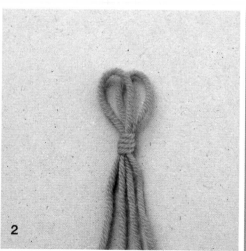

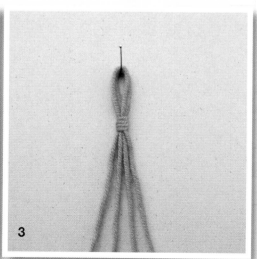

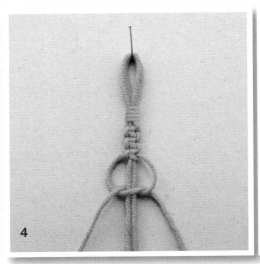
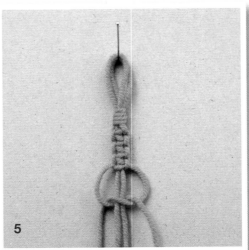
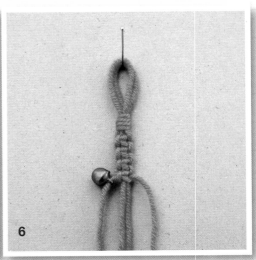

4 Tie four square knots. This technique requires adult help. Tying square knots may seem a little tricky at first, but once you have done it a dozen times you'll be sorted. Bring the right strand over the two middle strands. Then bring the left strand over the right strand, under the two middle strands and through the loop formed by the right strand. Pull the right and left strand until the knot tightens.

5 Bring the left strand over the two middle strands. Then bring the right strand over the left strand, under the two middle strands and through the loop formed by the left strand. Pull the right and left strand until the knot tightens. Yippee…you have tied a square knot! Repeat until you have tied four square knots.

6 Thread a bell on to the left-hand length of wool and tie two square knots. Repeat 13 times. Tie two square knots.

7 Trim the ends leaving about 6cm/2½in excess. Fasten the anklets as you would a friendship bracelet.

eco info

This project uses wool, which is a renewable resource. If you want to be extra eco-friendly, try unravelling old jumpers or scarves and re-using the wool to make these ankle bells.

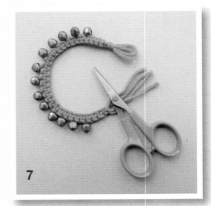

materials

- Long cardboard tube (a postal tube is ideal)
- Washable PVA glue
- Long strip of tin/aluminum foil
- Small cup of dried beans or uncooked rice
- Coloured paper
- Sticky tape

rainstick

The rainstick is a Peruvian instrument traditionally made from dried, hollow cacti. Luckily for us, you can make a pretty good version from an old postal tube and a few scoops of uncooked rice!

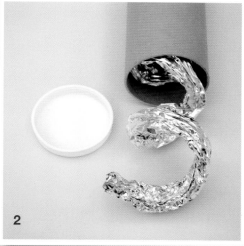

how-to

1 Seal one end of your tube. Postal tubes usually come with a plastic cap. If yours does, glue the cap in place. If it doesn't, use cardboard and tape instead.

2 Take a long piece of tin/aluminum foil that's about twice the length of your cardboard tube. Scrunch it up tightly to make a long snake shape. Push this snake into your tube, coiling it around like a spring as you go.

3 Pour the uncooked rice into the open end of your tube.

4 Seal the other end of your rainstick and decorate. We used cut paper but felt-tip pens or crayons are great too.

hints and tips

To play your rainstick, simply tip it to a 45-degree angle. As you tip the rainstick, turn it slightly to keep the sound going for a longer time. You can also use it as a shaker.

eco info

This craft uses household and recycled materials. Please always recycle your tin/aluminum foil after use!

bottle xylophone

Here is another great musical instrument you can make straight from your recycling bin. Children will love experimenting with the changing pitch as they increase or decrease the water level in each bottle.

how-to

1 Stand your bottles in a line and have your little helper fill them with water using a jug/pitcher and funnel. Add a little more water to each bottle as you move along the row.

2 Add a few drops of different coloured food colouring to each bottle. You can mix the food colouring if you want to make additional colours (this gives you a great excuse to talk about colour theory, too).

3 Give your little one a chopstick (or other wooden implement) and let them tap the bottles to discover the different sound each bottle makes.

hints and tips

When you tap your bottle xylophone, you will notice that more water produces a lower pitch and less water produces a higher pitch. But if you blow across the top of the bottle, rather than hitting it, you will see that the reverse is true!

1

2

3

ribbon rings

Kids love to dance and move to music, and it's even more fun when they have a funky ribbon ring to wave around at the same time. You can take the ribbon rings outside and watch them flutter in the breeze.

how-to

1 Start by cutting six lengths of ribbon. I used rainbow colours, but you can use whatever you have to hand. Each length of ribbon needs to be about 1m/40in long.

2 This step is for grown-ups only. Heat seal both ends of the ribbon with a lighter in order to prevent the ribbon from fraying. To do this, hold the end of the ribbon a couple of millimetres away from the flame until the edge of the ribbon starts to melt.

3 Fold one end of the ribbon through the ring and secure the fold with tightly wrapped thread. Repeat for each length of ribbon.

hints and tips

You can use silk ribbon instead of satin ribbon for a more floaty effect.

eco info

If you don't have spare curtain rings lying around the house, go on a hunt for the perfect stick instead.

materials

For each ring you will need:
- Satin ribbon, 16mm/⅝in wide (6m x 6½yd in total)
- Scissors • Thread
- Cigarette lighter
- One wooden curtain ring (6cm/2½in diameter)

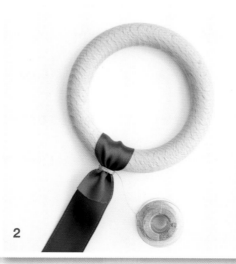

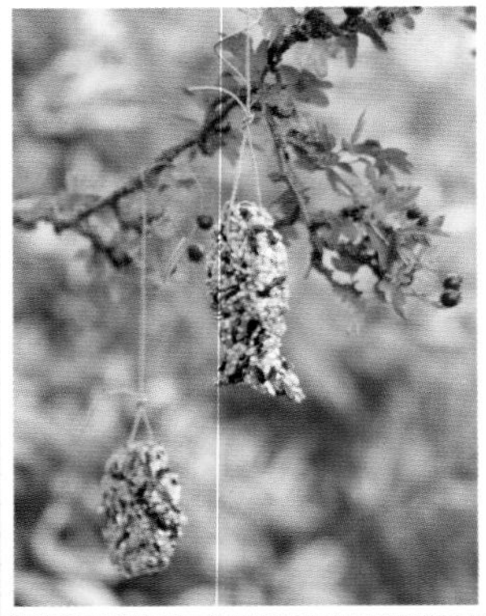

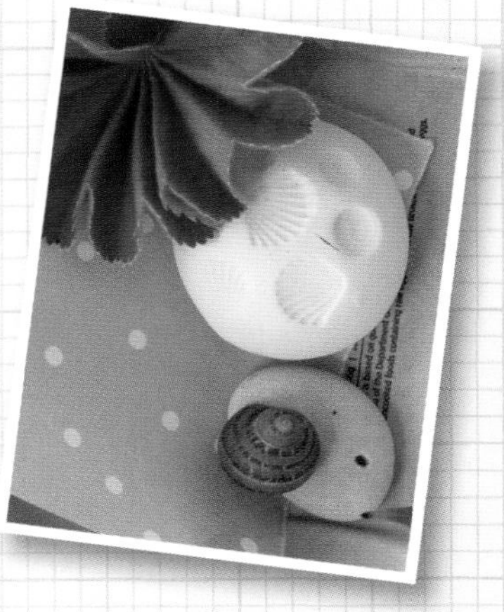

nature

seed bombs

Get your kids involved in a bit of guerrilla gardening and make some seed bombs with them. They are a perfect way to introduce new vegetation into forgotten or unloved public spaces.

materials

- 1 cup of air-drying modelling clay
- Container for mixing
- 1 cup of compost
- Water
- 2 packets of native wildflower seeds

how-to

1 Break the clay into small pieces then pop it into a mixing bowl along with the compost and a splash of water. Rub the clay into the compost with your hands or a fork until the two are well combined. This can be a messy job so make sure there is a bowl of soapy water on hand for a quick clean-up afterwards.

2 Sprinkle a couple of packets of native wildflower seeds into your clay/compost mix and gently mix.

3 Roll your mixture into small, grape-sized balls and put on a tray. Put the tray of seed bombs on a sunny windowsill to dry out. This usually takes 24–48 hours.

hints and tips

Do make sure you use a seed mix native to the country in which you live!

eco info

This craft uses natural materials and benefits the local environment.

1

2

3

nature stones

Going for a nature walk gives everyone a great excuse to get out of the house. Next time you go, pick up some natural treasures along the way. When you get home you can preserve their shape and texture in clay.

how-to

1 Go for a nature walk and collect lots of different items that might make interesting prints in the clay.

2 Cut your clay and roll each piece into an egg-sized ball.

3 Press each item into your clay ball to create a print and place the ball on a baking sheet.

4 Bake the nature stones according to the manufacturers' instructions on the packet of clay.

hints and tips

Bear in mind that the natural objects you choose will need to be robust enough to be pressed into a ball of clay. Items that might make good impressions are shells, flowers, leaves and seed pods.

eco info

This activity uses all natural materials.

materials
- Block of oven-bake modelling clay
- Knife
- Natural objects, such as leaves, flowers, seed pods or shells
- Flat baking sheet
- Oven mitt

1

2

3

4

bug house

Kids love bugs (sometimes a little bit too much!), so why not give the bugs a bit of lovin' back and make them their very own home.

materials
- Old wooden box
- Drill • String/twine• Ruler
- Bamboo cane and sticks
- Saw • Cardboard • Craft knife

1

2

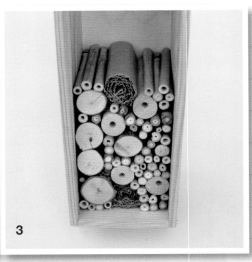

3

how-to

1 To make a handle, drill two holes in the top of the box and thread some string through (grown-ups only). The box will be considerably heavier when finished, so make sure the handle will be strong enough to support the weight.

2 This step is for grown-ups only. Measure the depth of your box. Now, using a handsaw or circular saw, cut your sticks and cane to the same length. Next, cut your cardboard to fit the depth of the box and roll up. The number of sticks and cardboard rolls you need depends on the size of your box.

3 Now your little helper can begin to fill the box up with the cut pieces of cane, sticks and cardboard. Keep going until the box is completely packed.

4 Hang, or sit, your bug house in a dry sheltered space and wait for your insect friends to move in.

eco info

This activity uses natural and recycled materials and benefits the local environment and wildlife.

walnut Shell boats

I just adore these little boats. You can take them to your nearest stream for their maiden voyage or, if you want to stay closer to home, the washing up bowl will do just fine.

how-to

1 Using a nutcracker, carefully crack some walnuts in two. Try to crack the nut around the middle where there is a raised ridge. This way, the nut should crack neatly into two halves.

2 Roll a ball of plasticine that's small enough to fit into a walnut half and push this onto one end of the skewer. Take the small rectangle of paper and punch a hole at either end, about 5mm/¼in in from the edge. Now gently thread the paper onto the mast.

3 Push the plasticine ball firmly into the base of a walnut shell. Now you're all ready to go sailing!

materials
- Whole walnuts
- Nutcracker
- Plasticine/Blu-Tack
- Toothpick/wooden skewer (cut into 8cm/3in lengths)
- Paper (5 x 4cm/2 x 1½in)
- Hole punch

1

2

3

easy birdfeeder

If the weather outside is frightful, why not make some munchies for your feathered friends. They are great fun to make and the birds will love you for it.

materials

- Jug/pitcher or bowl for mixing
- Gelatin • ½ cup of water
- I cup of birdseed • Fork
- Cookie cutters • Vegetable oil
- Wooden skewer • Twine or ribbon

1

2

3

4

how-to

1 Make up your gelatin according to packet instructions. For this recipe you need half a cup. Leave the mixture to stand until it starts to congeal. Add your birdseed to the congealed gelatin. Mix together briskly using a fork until the birdseed is well coated.

2 Rub the inside of your cookie cutters with a little oil. Then, using a fork, press the mixture into your cookie cutters. Pop your moulds in the fridge and leave them to set for an hour or two.

3 Carefully remove your birdfeeders from the cookie cutter moulds and leave them on a plate to dry completely. This usually takes about 2 days at room temperature.

4 Once your birdfeeders have dried, make a small hole in the centre of each birdfeeder with a wooden skewer, thread through a length of twine, and hang in a tree.

hints and tips

When you hang your birdfeeder, make sure it is in a sheltered area as rainwater will dissolve the gelatin. If you want your feeder to be waterproof, use lard as a substitute for the gelatin; simply melt the lard and pour it over the birdseed then pack it into a muffin pan to set.

eco info

This project provides our feathered friends with much-needed food during the winter months.

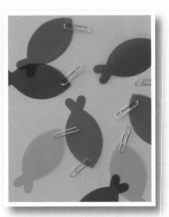

recycling bin

kaleidoscope

Kaleidoscopes are timeless toys and you can make a great one from household scraps. Kids will be fascinated by the wonderful colours and shapes they spy inside.

how-to

1 Using a hammer and nail, pierce a hole in the metallic end of the tube (this step is for grown-ups only).

2 Create a reflective prism by cutting your mirror card into three strips (grown-ups only). The strips should be 2cm/¾in shorter than the length of your tube. To calculate the width of your strips, measure the diameter of your tube and multiply it by 0.866. Using sticky tape, stick the three strips of mirror card together to form a triangular prism.

3 Push the prism into your tube so that it is flush at one end. Secure in place using sticky tape.

materials

- Clean, empty cookie or potato-chip tube
- Hammer • Nail
- Double-sided mirror card (or aluminum foil glued onto card)
- Scissors • Ruler
- Sticky tape
- Transparent plastic (from the recycling bin)
- Pencil • Tracing paper
- Small colourful transparent objects, such as beads

1

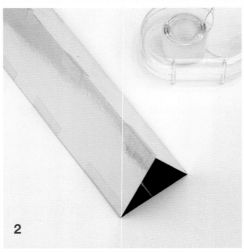

2

3

4 Stand the tube on top of a piece of transparent plastic and, using a pencil, draw around the outside of the tube. Cut out the circle of transparent plastic and place it on top of the prism. Tape into place. Pour your beads on top of the transparent plastic. Be careful not to overfill as the beads need to be able to move around.

5 Stand the tube on top of a piece of tracing paper and, using a pencil, draw around the outside of the tube. Cut out the circle of tracing paper and use it to line the plastic lid for your tube to create a frosted effect.

6 Put the lid back on the end of the tube. You can secure the lid using some tape or glue. Once your kaleidoscope is complete let your little one decorate it using paper, felt pens/markers and crayons.

hints and tips

• Before you make your kaleidoscope, send your little one on a treasure hunt around the house to find lots of small, colourful (preferably transparent) objects to put inside the object chamber.
• If you don't have an old biscuit/potato chip tube you can improvise and make one from an old kitchen roll tube instead.

eco info

This project demonstrates the importance of reusing materials that still have a useful life, rather than throwing them in the bin.

4

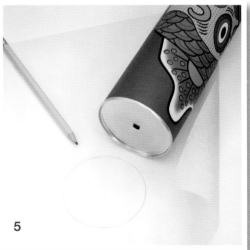

5

6

marble maze

If you have any nuts and bolts left over from DIY projects, this marble maze is a brilliant way to use them up. Once your little one has mastered the current maze, you can move the rubber bands around to create a new one!

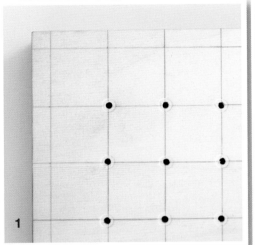

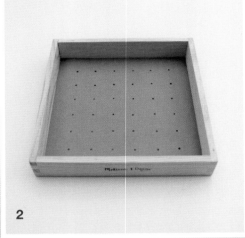

how-to

1 Using a pencil and ruler, mark out a grid on the underside of your box. The number of squares in the grid will be dependent upon the size of the box. As a general rule, each grid square needs to measure about 3cm/1¼in².

2 Carefully drill a hole at each intersection on the grid. (Grown-ups only!)

3 Working on the back of the box, push a bolt into each hole then screw on the nut on the inside of the box to hold the bolt in place.

4 Now attach rubber bands to the bolts to form a maze. If you need inspiration, then search for a 'maze generator' on the internet and you will find a program that will generate a pattern that you can follow.

5 Use some stickers to define the start and end point in the maze. Then pop the marble in and play!

hints and tips

If you are running short on time or don't have a suitable wooden box you can make a marble maze from a cardboard box instead. To do this, cut down the sides of the box to create a shallow tray, then position thick drinking straws on the base of the box to create the walls of the maze. You can fix the straws into place with sticky tape or glue. Quick and easy!

eco info

This project uses up all those rubber bands the postman/mailman always seems to drop!

materials

- Old wooden box (shallow boxes work better)
- Pencil
- Ruler
- Drill and 3mm drillbit
- Nuts and 3mm bolts
- Rubber bands
- Stickers
- Marbles

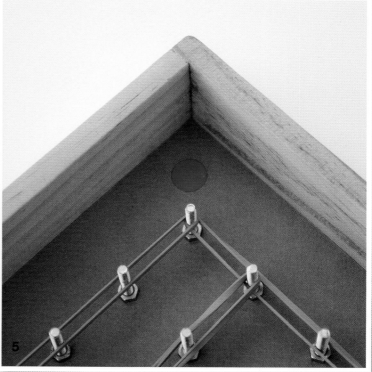

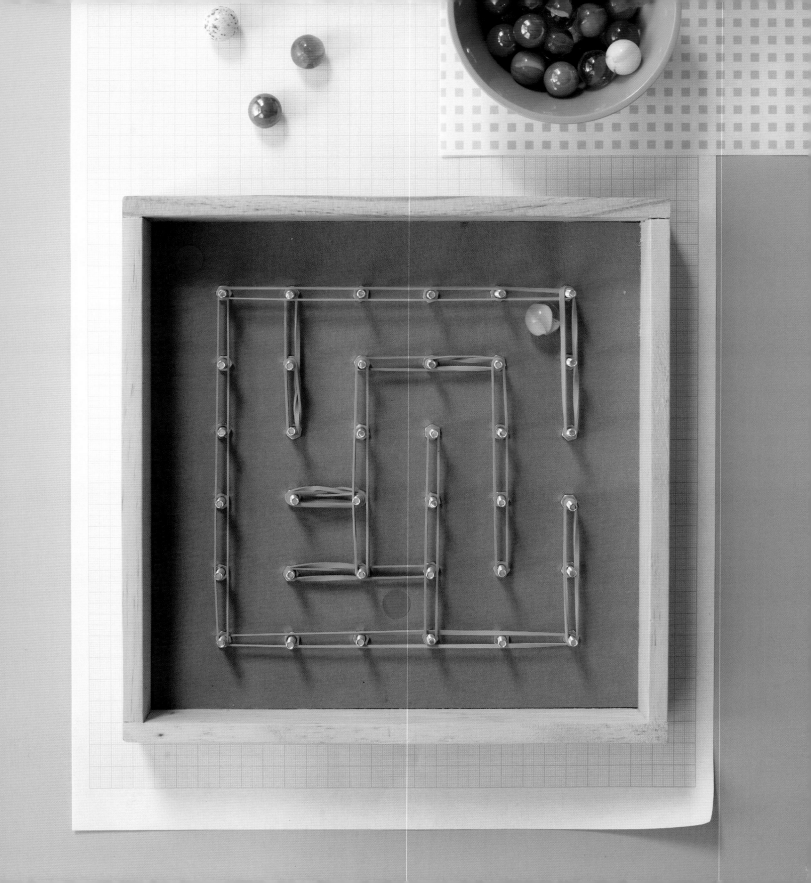

paper cup popper

Pompom poppers are great fun and fantastic for hand/eye co-ordination. Even better, you can whip one up in no time at all – great for children's parties or a rainy afternoon.

how-to

1 Carefully cut out the base from your paper cup using a craft knife or a pair of scissors. (This step is for grown-ups only.)

2 Tie a knot in your uninflated balloon. Using scissors, cut a small opening at the other end.

3 Stretch the balloon over the base of your paper cup. You may wish to add a rubber band to hold the balloon firmly in place.

4 To play with your popper, place the pompom in the base of your cup and pull the knotted end of the balloon.

When you let go, the pompom will fly out of the cup. Try to catch it in the cup as it falls back down to earth.

hints and tips

If you don't have any pompoms handy, make balls from screwed-up paper. It's better to use something lightweight; that way your little one is not likely to leave a dent in your ceiling...or somebody's head!

eco info

This project is a good way to reuse take-away paper coffee cups. First wash and dry them, then cover the outside with scraps of giftwrap from the recycling bin.

1

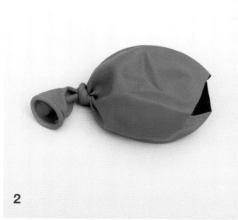

2

3

magnetic fishing game

Fishing games are easy to make and great fun for playing with in the bath or paddling pool. Use the fishing rod to catch as many of the slippery paperclip fish as you can.

how-to

1 Find a stick to use as your fishing rod. Cut the stick to size, sandpaper the ends and shave off any knobbles with a craft knife. Drill a small hole in one end of the stick. (This step is for grown-ups only.)

2 Thread the wire or thread through the hole in the stick and wrap it around the stick to secure.

3 Tie the other end of the thread or wire to the magnet.

4 Photocopy the fish template on page 119. Cut out the template and place it onto a piece of coloured acetate or scrap plastic. Draw around the fish shape then cut it out.

5 Punch a hole in the 'nose' end of each fish and thread through a paperclip.

hints and tips

• This project uses coloured acetate, but scrap plastic, thin card or cardboard from the recycling bin works just as well. If you are using cardboard, remember you won't be able to play the game in the bath!

• Shortening the string will make the game easier for younger kids.

• Please remember to supervise your kids around water at all times.

materials

• Thin stick • Saw
• Sandpaper
• Craft knife/scissors
• Drill
• 50cm/20in length of strong thread (or string/wool)
• Magnet (we used a neodymium ring magnet)
• Coloured acetate sheets • Pencil
• Paperclips
• Hole punch

4

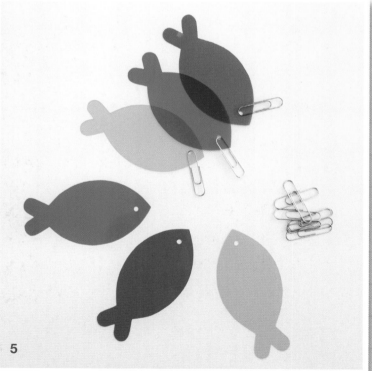

5

bubble discovery bottle

If you have a budding scientist on your hands, this discovery bottle will be a real hit. It's great fun to make and intriguing to play with. Shake the bottle and watch the colourful bubbles fill the bottle.

materials
- Small transparent plastic bottles
- Water
- Washing-up liquid
- Food colouring
- Electrical tape

how-to

1 Pour about 2.5cm/1in of water into the bottom of your clean plastic bottle. Add a generous squirt of washing-up liquid.

2 Now add a few drops of food colouring. Vibrant red or green both work well.

3 Screw the lid tightly onto the bottle. Wrap electrical tape around the lid to prevent it from coming off. Shake the bottle to make lots of colourful bubbles.

hints and tips

• When making your discovery bottles, make sure you use small plastic bottles as they are much easier for kids to hold and manipulate.

• These discovery bottles also make great toys for babies (with the exception of the magnetic bottle). If you are worried about the lids coming off, then glue them into place with a hot glue-gun before applying the tape.

more discovery bottles

From a gloopy bottle full of glitter to a bubbly ocean scene, there are so many different discovery bottles you and your little helper can make.

glitter bottle

Pour liquid glucose syrup into your bottle until it is ¼ full. Add ½ tbsp of glitter. Screw the lid tightly onto the bottle. Wrap electrical tape around the lid to prevent it from coming off. Turn the bottle and watch the glittery mixture slowly ooze around the inside of the bottle.

ocean bottle

Pour water into bottle until it is ⅓ full. Add a few drops of blue food colouring to the water. Pour baby oil or cooking oil into the bottle until it is about ⅔ full and then drop in a toy boat or fish. Screw the lid tightly onto the bottle. Wrap electrical tape around the lid to prevent it from coming off. As you turn the bottle you will see the waves gently roll. You can also shake the bottle to mix the oil and water and then watch the two separate.

electrostatic bottle

Cut up some small squares of tissue paper. Alternately you can use polystyrene balls or regular polystyrene broken up into small pieces. Put the tissue paper/polystyrene in the bottle. Do not add any water! Screw the lid tightly onto the bottle. Wrap electrical tape around the lid to prevent it from coming off. Rub the outside of the bottle on your clothes and watch all the pieces of tissue paper/polystyrene cling to the sides of the bottle!

magnetic bottle

Put a handful of small metal objects such as paperclips, pins, nuts and old jewellery into an empty bottle. Screw the lid tightly onto the bottle. Wrap electrical tape around the lid to prevent it from coming off. Rub a large magnet around the outside of the bottle to manipulate the objects on the inside.

eco info

This project is a great use for all those plastic water bottles that mount up in the recycling bin.

cardboard castle

This cardboard castle is a great gift to make, it won't cost the earth and your little one can have a great deal of fun customizing the outside before playing with it.

how-to

1 Photocopy the castle templates on page 116–118 and then cut them all out.

2 Place each template on a scrap piece of corrugated cardboard then draw around it using a pencil.

3 Cut the castle shapes and the slits out using a metal ruler and craft knife (this step is for grown-ups only).

4 Once you have cut out all the shapes, slot them together to create the castle as shown.

hints and tips

Once your castle is complete, let your little one decorate it. Stick to felt pens/markers or crayons because paint will make the box go soggy.

eco info

This project is a great use for a large cardboard box of the type that new appliances or pieces of furniture are delivered in.

materials
- Scrap paper
- Pencil • Scissors
- Scrap corrugated cardboard
- Craft knife
- Metal ruler
- Felt pens/markers
- Crayons

paper and card

shadow makers

These shadow makers give your little ones a good excuse to run round the house in the dark with a torch/flashlight in hand. They work just as well in front of a sunny window too.

materials

- Scissors/craft knife
- Coloured card
- Pencil
- Sticky tape
- Wooden lollipop sticks/coffee stirrers
- Torch/flashlight

how-to

1 Photocopy the templates on page 120. Cut out the templates and place them onto a piece of card then draw around the shapes.

2 Cut out the shapes using a craft knife (grown-ups only) or a pair of scissors.

3 Use a piece of sticky tape to attach a sturdy wooden stick to the back of each shape.

4 Pull the curtains and use a torch/flashlight to project the shapes onto the wall.

hints and tips

If your little one is keen to put on their own productions why not help them to make their own shadow puppet theatre? All you need is a big cardboard box, a white sheet and a lamp. Once rehearsals have finished, make a big bowl of popcorn and round up some family members to watch the show!

eco info

Be even more eco-friendly and use a wind up torch/flashlight!

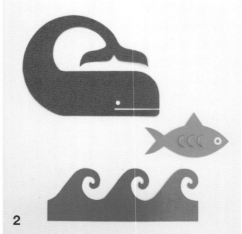

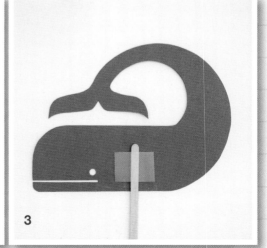

jar of love

This little 'jar of love' is a fun gift for your kids to make for their loved ones. Roll up a sheet of paper containing a special message or an original piece of artwork and pop it in the jar.

how-to

1 Take an old jar and soak the label off using warm water. Dry thoroughly.

2 Cut a piece of paper (grown-ups only), no higher than the jar, and get your little one to write or draw a special message on it. Roll the piece of paper up and tie with some pretty thread.

3 Pop your message in the jar, along with some coloured confetti, glitter and any other keepsakes you wish to add. Screw on lid and give to a loved one.

materials

- Small glass jar
- Water
- Sheet of white paper
- Scissors
- Pens or coloured pencils
- Thread
- Paper confetti
- Glitter

eco info

Homemade gifts made from recycled items are much more eco-friendly than store-bought ones!

1

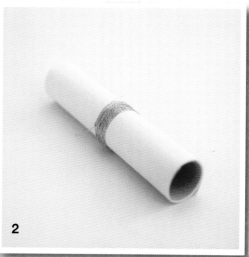

2

3

catapult plane

These catapult planes are fantastic for improving hand-to-eye co-ordination. When your little one has got the knack of it, get ready to duck – the planes can fly a long way!

materials

- A5/½ letter size sheet of paper
- Hole punch
- Rubber bands
- Wooden lollipop/craft sticks

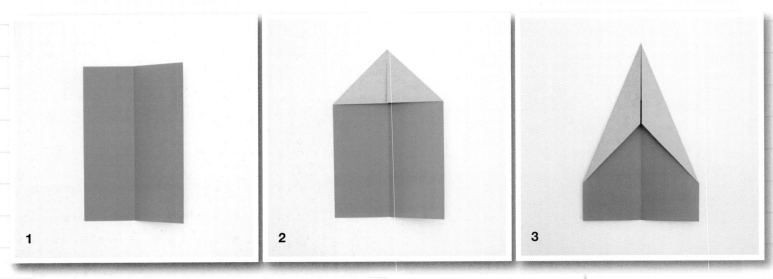

1

2

3

how-to

1 Fold the sheet of paper in half along the length. Crease sharply and unfold.

2 Using the photograph above as a guide, fold the top corners down to meet on the centre line and crease.

3 Fold the two edges against the centre line, as shown.

4 Make a mountain fold along the centre line (so that the crease faces upwards).

5 Create two wing creases on either side by folding the

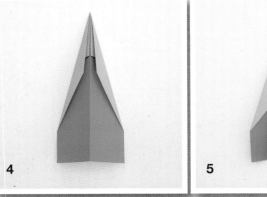

4

5

long edges into the centre so that the end of the folds meets the base of the mountain fold. Crease.

6 Punch a hole in the bottom of the plane as shown in the photograph, below.

7 Pinch the sides of the rubber band together then push the looped end through the hole in the paper plane. Pull the other end of the rubber band through the loop and carefully pull tight.

8 Wooden lollipop/craft sticks make great launchers. Wrap a different-coloured rubber band around the top of the stick to act as a marker. Loop the plane's rubber band over the top of the stick, pull the plane back until the rubber is taut, and let go.

hints and tips

• Your little ones can have a lot of fun decorating their paper planes. Just remember to avoid anything that might make the paper go soggy.
• When it's time to launch your planes bear in mind that they can fire a long way. For best results (and to avoid any breakages or injuries) get outdoors!

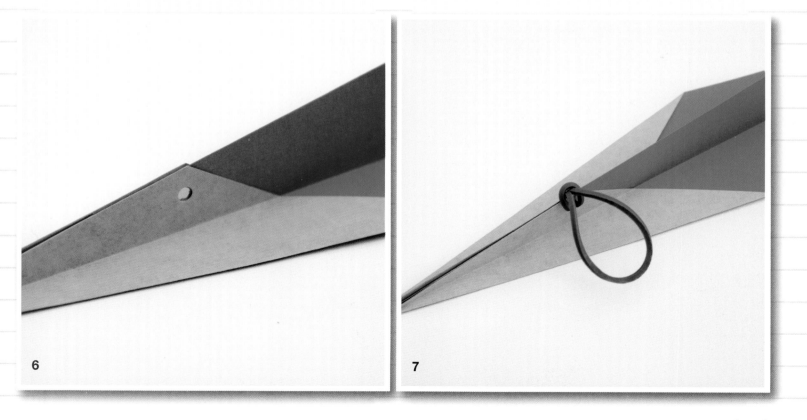

6

7

Pac-man mobile

Feeling a bit retro? If so, make a Pac-Man mobile for your little ones' room and introduce them to an '80s icon. Hang the mobile from the ceiling and watch the friendly ghosts hover in the air.

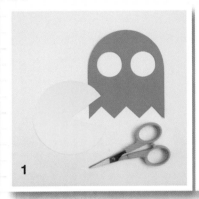

how-to

1 Photocopy the Pac-Man and ghost templates on page 121. Cut out the templates and place them onto pieces of coloured card. Draw around the templates and cut them out using a pair of scissors (kids) or a craft knife (grown-ups only). You will need to cut out a front and a back shape in the same colour for each Pac-Man and ghost character.

2 Take one of the ghost shapes and lay a piece of clear plastic over the holes where the eyes will go. Tape into place. Cut out two circles of black card for each of the eyes and centre on plastic. Tape/glue into place.

3 Tape a 20cm/8in length of cotton to the back piece of each of your characters. Place the front shape on top of the back shape and tape or glue into place.

4 Place a drinking straw vertically on a flat surface and tie a ghost to each end of the straw. Next, tie your Pac-Man to the centre of a drinking straw. Attach two different lengths of cotton to either end of the straw and tie on the ghost straws.

hints and tips

Get creative with your mobile shapes and hang a moon and stars or simple flowers or cars. If your little one is a budding artist why not ask them to draw their own template and choose their own coloured papers.

eco info

This craft uses recycled paper.

materials
- Card (red, orange, blue, yellow and black)
- Pencil
- Scissors/craft knife
- Clear scrap plastic/acetate
- Double-sided/glue
- Thick cotton
- Drinking straws

paper jumping beans

These paper jumping beans are a homemade version of the childhood classic. Your little helper can have fun drawing faces and shapes on the beans. Make sure you make lots because everyone will want a go.

materials
- Pencil
- Scissors
- Pieces of thin card
- Crayon or pen
- Sticky tape
- Marbles

how-to

1 Photocopy the template on page 119. Cut out the template and place it onto a piece of thin card. Draw around the template then cut it out (grown-ups only). Bring your jumping bean to life by drawing a face right in the middle of the template as shown, below.

2 Place the card shape face down on a flat surface. Fold in each side section as indicated on the template.

3 Now fold up one long end and bring it to meet the side tabs. Fix it in place using sticky tape.

4 (*See picture overleaf*) Next, place a marble inside the jumping bean.

5 (*See picture overleaf*) Fold up the other long end and stick it in place. Use sticky tape to reinforce the join.

eco info

This is a great way to give old marbles a new lease of life.

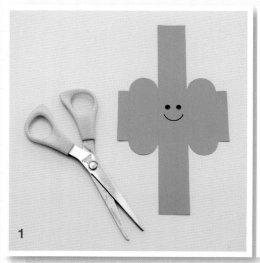

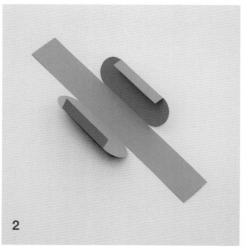

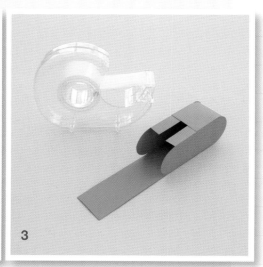

hints and tips

• Your little ones can have a lot of fun decorating their jumping beans. Just remember to do this before cutting and folding the bean and try to avoid anything that might make the paper go soggy!

• When it's time to test out your jumping beans you can experiment with how different surfaces affect the movement of the jumping beans. Do tilted, flat, rough or smooth surfaces make the beans go faster?

• If you want to make some 'super grippy' jumping beans why not make them from a sheet of fine sandpaper instead of card.

did you know?

• Real jumping beans are native to Mexico and grow on the jumping bean shrub (*Sebastiana pavoniana*).

• The beans themselves are actually seedpods through which the larva of a small grey moth has chewed. After consuming the seed within the seedpod, the moth larva throws itself, with great force, from one side of the capsule to another, causing the capsule to 'jump'.

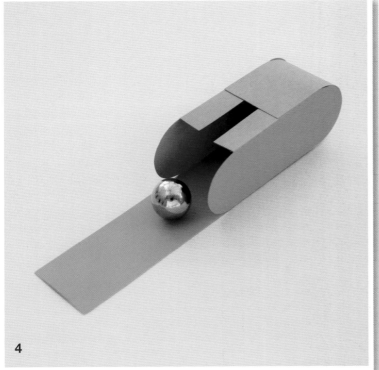

4

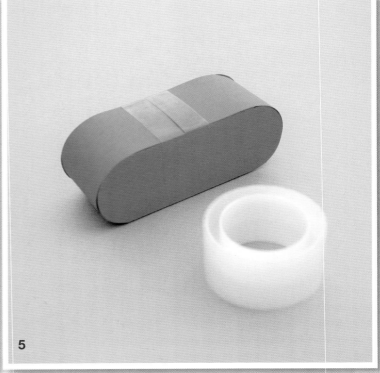

5

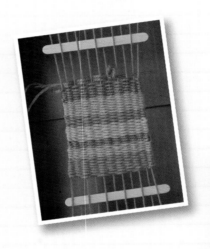

sewing
and
threading

paper bead necklace

There is something really therapeutic about making paper beads and they make great threading practice for little hands. You might love them so much that you decide to make a stash just for yourself!

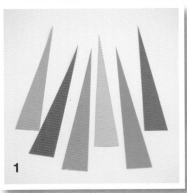

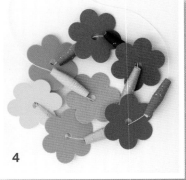

how-to

1 Take a piece of origami paper measuring 15 x 15cm/ 6 x 6in and mark out 20–30 triangles measuring 15 x 2cm/6 x 1in. Cut them out using scissors (kids) or a craft knife and metal ruler (grown-ups only!).

2 Starting with the flat end of the triangle, wind the paper tightly around the pencil or skewer. When you have about 2cm/1in of paper left to roll, pop a dab of glue on the point of the triangle and carry on winding.

3 Hold the point in place until the glue sets. Carefully slide the bead off the skewer and leave it to dry.

4 Once you have made approximately 20–30 beads, cut a length of strong thread and start to thread them on, alternating the beads with cut-out flowers.

hints and tips

- If you have a patient pre-schooler, they will have no problem making their own beads with a little help from you. Make sure they use a pencil rather than a skewer and begin by wrapping the paper around for them. Then, let them roll the pencil along the table to wind the rest of the paper up and blob on the glue at the end.
- You can coat your beads in an acrylic glaze if you want them to last longer.
- The cut-out paper flowers were made using a craft punch but you can buy similar ones from craft stores.
- If you don't have time to make the rolled paper beads, try threading cut straws instead.

Cardboard box loom

Learning to weave does not require expensive equipment. All you need is a sturdy cardboard box, some scraps of wool in bright primary colours and the boundless enthusiasm of a little kid!

how-to

1 Begin by marking out holes along the two short edges of the box. Measure the box and make a mark at the centre point. Then mark 5 points either side of the centre point, each one about 1cm/½in apart. Now pierce a hole through each point using a sharp darning needle.

2 Thread the darning needle with a long piece of wool and tie a knot at the end. Starting at the right hand side, thread the wool through all the holes in the box. When you reach the end, tighten any loose threads before tying off. This wool, running lengthwise, is called the warp.

3 Thread the darning needle with another length of wool and start to weave it over and under the warp threads, making sure you alternate on each row. The threads that go from side to side across the loom are called the weft.

4 Real looms use something called a 'reed' to compress each row as it is woven. We used a lollipop/craft stick instead, and it worked really well!

hints and tips

- Small fingers may find it easier to weave with a lollipop/craft stick rather than a darning needle. Pierce a hole in one end of the stick and thread through the wool, then pass the stick through the warp threads.
- This project works best if the marking of the holes and piercing of the cardboard is left to you. Then you can help your little one with the threading and weaving.

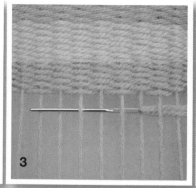

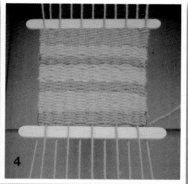

sock hobby horse

This super-cute hobby horse is made from an old sock and a broom handle. The project is best carried out by a grown up, but when finished it makes a perfect handmade gift for any little kid with a big imagination!

how-to

1 To make the horse's eyes, cut out two circles of felt, each one approximately 3cm/1¼in in diameter. In the middle of each circle cut a small slit (grown-ups only) and push the plastic toy eye through the slit in the felt.

2 Using the point of a pair of scissors (grown-ups only) make small holes in the sock where you want the eyes to be positioned. Now push the eyes through the holes and fix them securely in place using their plastic washers.

3 Push the stuffing into the sock. To avoid a floppy head make sure you pack in as much as you can. Use a ruler to push the stuffing right to the end of the sock.

4 (*See picture overleaf*) To make the horse's ear, photocopy the template on page 122. Cut it out and place it on a piece of felt. Draw around the template twice then cut out two ears.

5 (*See picture overleaf*) Pleat the felt ears as indicated on the paper template and pin them to the sides of the horse's head. Using a needle and thread, sew the ears securely in place.

1

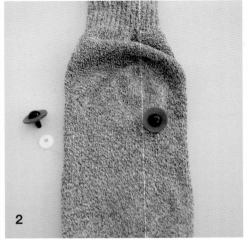
2

3

6 To make the mane, fold a 10cm/4in square of cardboard in half. Wind a length of wool around the card. Then, using sharp scissors (grown-ups only), cut through the wrapped loops along the gap in the cardboard.

7 Using a darning needle, pull a length of wool through the sock on the back of the horse's head. Remove the needle and knot the wool into place. Repeat this process until your horse has a good mane of hair. This process is

very easy but can take a bit of time, so it's the perfect thing to do in front of the TV when the kids are in bed!

8 Cut some lengths of rickrack for the bridle, and, using a needle and thread, sew into place as shown. Add a jingle bell on either side of the head.

9 Place the sock head over the end of the broomstick and bind it in place using thick twine or rubber bands.

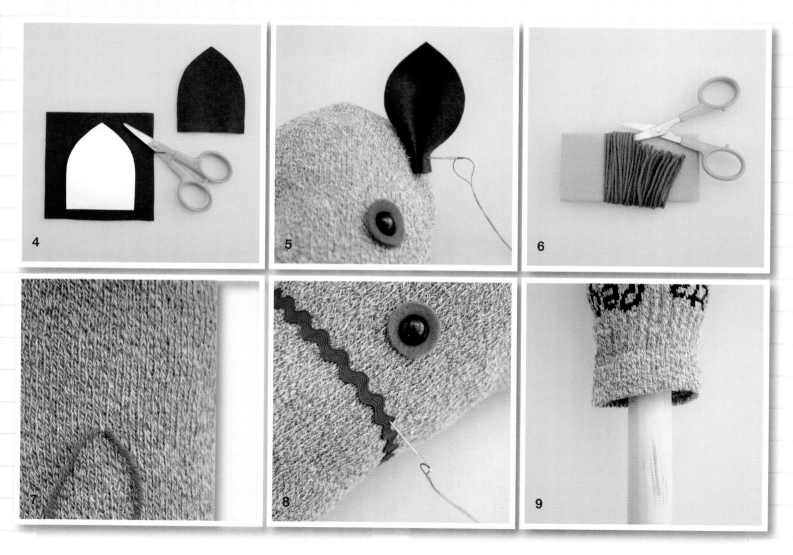

threaded paper garland

Geometric shapes are really fashionable at the moment and this cheerful rainbow-bright garland will look really cool hanging up in any kids' bedroom. The garlands also make great party decorations.

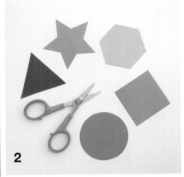

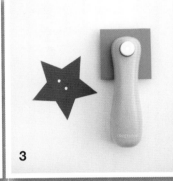

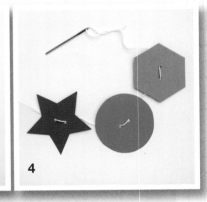

how-to

1 Photocopy the geometric shape templates on page 123. Cut out the templates and place them on pieces of coloured card. Draw around the shapes using a pencil.

2 Cut out the shapes using a craft knife and metal ruler (grown-ups only) or a pair of scissors. For every metre of garland you will need about 16 shapes.

3 Punch two regularly spaced holes exactly in the centre of each shape.

4 Thread a darning needle with a long piece of wool, tie a knot at the end and start to thread on the shapes. If you don't have a needle, wrap a piece of sticky tape around the end of a length of wool and use that instead.

hints and tips

Threading is great for developing fine motor skills.

materials
- Scissors • Pencil
- Thin card in rainbow colours • Craft knife
- Metal ruler • Hole punch
- Darning needle
- Wool or cotton thread for threading
- Sticky tape (optional)

sewing cards

Sewing and threading is a fun activity that's great for honing fine motor skills and improving hand-eye coordination. These jolly cards are always useful to have in your bag when you are out and about.

materials

- Scissors/craft knife
- Pencil or pen
- Thin card • Hole punch
- Shoelaces/wool
- Blunt darning needle (optional)
- Pipe cleaner/chenille stem (optional)

how-to

1 Photocopy the sewing card template on page 122. Use scissors (kids) or a craft knife (grown-ups only) to cut out the template. Place it onto a thin piece of card, draw around the shape and carefully cut it out.

2 Draw a smiley face in the centre of the card.

3 Use a hole punch to make holes at regular intervals all the way around the perimeter of the sewing card.

4 Shoelaces are perfect for your little ones to 'sew' with.

hints and tips

• If you don't have any shoelaces, use a long piece of wool instead, winding a little sticky tape around the end to create a 'point' and to prevent the wool from fraying.

• Older kids could use a large darning needle, or make their own 'needle' from a pipe cleaner/chenille stem.

eco info

If you are short of time, you can make great sewing cards from cereal packets rescued from the recycling bin or old greeting cards. Just cut out interesting shapes and punch some holes at regular intervals around the perimeter. Easy!

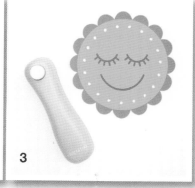

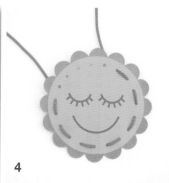

science

magic potion

This is a fabulous colour-changing experiment that your little one will want to try again and again! It's so easy to do and uses only natural foodstuffs that you are likely to have in your fridge.

materials

- Red cabbage
- Knife and chopping board
- Microwavable container
- Water
- Mixing bowl
- Sieve
- Several small white containers, such as old jars or yoghurt pots
- Pipette (or medicine dropper)
- Lemon juice (fresh or bottled)

how-to

1 Put a handful of roughly chopped red cabbage into a microwavable container and cover it with water. Microwave on full power for two minutes then let the mixture stand until the water has turned blue.

2 When the blue water has cooled, sieve it into a mixing bowl. Decant the blue liquid into smaller containers for the experiment. We keep a stockpile of glass jars and yoghurt pots in the house for occasions such as this! Pour some lemon juice into a bowl then use a pipette to squeeze a few drops of the juice into each pot. Watch the blue water turn the most incredible shade of pink!

how it works

Red cabbage contains a pigment molecule called anthocyanin. Anthocyanin is a natural pH indicator that changes colour according to the acidity of the solution. Very acidic solutions, such as lemon juice, will turn the anthocyanin a red/pink colour, whereas basic solutions will turn the anthocyanin blue/green.

eco info

This craft uses natural materials and is entirely non-toxic but please don't be tempted to taste it!

coloured flowers

As well as being quite magical, this classic science experiment demonstrates the way in which water travels through a plant in a process known as transpiration.

how-to

1 Trim the stem of your flower to fit in your glass jar. Next, make a slanted cut at the base of the stem (under running water if possible).

2 Pour warm water into your jar until it is ¾ full. Add food colouring to the water. You need approximately 20–30 drops of food colouring for each half cup of water.

3 Place the flower in the coloured water. The petals should start to take on colour after a few hours. Best results are achieved after 24–48 hours.

materials

- White long-stemmed flowers such as carnations
- Scissors
- Several glass jars
- Food colouring
- Warm water

hints and tips

You can create an amazing bi-coloured flower by slitting the stem of your flower up the middle and putting each side into a separate jar of coloured water.

invisible ink

Got a budding secret agent on your hands? Why not help them to make (and reveal) their own secret messages.

how-to

1 If you are using a fresh lemon, squeeze some of the juice into a bowl.

2 Dip your cotton bud into the lemon juice and write a message onto a sheet of white paper. Try not to use too much juice. Now allow the paper to dry thoroughly.

3 You can reveal your invisible message by either ironing the piece of paper (grown-ups only, please!) or by waving a hot hairdryer over it.

materials

- Lemon juice (fresh or bottled)
- Bowl
- Cotton buds/Q-tips or small paintbrush
- White paper
- Iron/hairdryer

how it works

Lemon juice is acidic and weakens the paper. When the paper is heated, the remaining acid turns the writing brown before discolouring the rest of the paper.

eco info

This experiment uses all-natural, non-toxic materials.

1

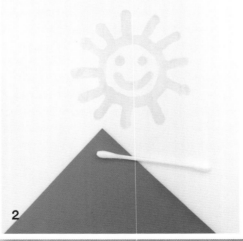

2

3

materials

- 1–2 cups of cornflour/cornstarch
- 1 cup water • Spoon
- Food colouring (optional)

oobleck

Is it a solid…is it a liquid…? No, it's Oobleck! Oobleck gets its name from a Dr. Seuss story called *Bartholomew and the Oobleck* in which a green, gluey goo falls from the sky and gums up everything in sight.

how-to

1 Pop 1 cup of cornflour/cornstarch into a mixing bowl. Pour a cup of water into the cornflour/cornstarch, mixing as you go. You can use a spoon for the mixing, but hands work just as well.

2 You may need to add more cornflour/cornstarch to the mix to achieve the perfect consistency. The mixture you are aiming to achieve should be fairly thick and will harden if you tap on it. If you pick the mixture up and squeeze it, it will form a ball but if you lay your hand flat the ball will lose its shape and run through your fingers.

3 Once your Oobleck is the perfect consistency you can add a few drops of food colouring.

hints and tips

• This is a messy activity, so make sure you wear appropriate clothes and have a bowl of soapy water on stand by for a quick clean up.
• Remember not to pour Oobleck down your drain!
• There are lots of ways you can experiment with your Oobleck. Try squeezing the mixture to form a ball. Now lay your ball on your open palm…what happens? Move your fingers through the mixture slowly; now try to move them quickly. Slowly lower your hands into the Oobleck. Now try to remove them quickly.

boredom busters

It's always great to have a few ideas up your sleeve in case of a boredom emergency. Here is a selection of fun, easy ideas that you can pull together in no time to keep little ones happy and out of mischief! If you are super-lucky you might even get five minutes to grab a quiet cuppa!

sensory play

- Pour a bag of rice or pasta shapes into a big, deep container. Get out some smaller jugs, tumblers and bowls. Perfect for scooping, pouring and measuring.
- Fill balloons with playdough and tie the ends securely to create fascinatingly squashy stress balls.

messy fun

- On a sunny day, take a jug of water outside and make mud pies in the back garden.
- Make some cloud dough: combine 8 cups of flour with one cup of baby oil for squidgy fun.
- A bag of flour + a bowl + a sieve = hours of fun!

crazy art

- Create bubble prints. Stir together ½ cup of water, 2 tablespoons of paint, and 1 tablespoon of washing-up liquid in a shallow, wide plastic bowl. Gently blow into the mixture using a straw until bubbles start to ooze out of the top of the bowl. Carefully lay a piece of paper on top of the cup to create the print.

- Ice-cube painting. Add a few drops of food colouring to water and freeze it in ice-cube trays. Once they are frozen, pop the cubes out and have fun painting with them on a big sheet of paper.
- Create a marshmallow and toothpick sculpture.
- Make a Paper Me. Stick together enough pieces of paper to make one piece that's big enough for your little (or not-so-little) one to lie down on. Now take a thick pen and draw all the way around him or her. Once your child get up, you'll be left with a life-sized body shape for them to decorate however they like!
- Make a play mat. Get a large piece of paper, place on the floor and draw in roads, traffic lights, houses, rivers and shops. Then get your toy cars out and let them zoom all the way around the 'town'.

science

- Make a volcano! Place an empty baby food jar on a tray. Surround the jar with playdough and mould it to look like a mountain. Put a drop of red food coloring and a tablespoon of baking soda in the jar. Then add some vinegar to it and stand clear as it erupts!
- Raisin Rising: Pour clear carbonated soda water into a clear glass. Drop four or five raisins into the glass. Watch and see how the air bubbles make the raisins rise and fall.
- Get to work cleaning old copper coins using a mixture of vinegar and salt and scrubbing with an old toothbrush.

nature & outdoor fun

• Collect a selection of natural objects – shells, roots or seeds, for example – for a nature table.
• Adopt a pet snail…but remember to let him go again at the end of the afternoon.
• Try some outdoor water painting. Simply use a cup of water and a paintbrush – great on a dry sunny day!
• When it's raining, go worm collecting. Put on your rubber boots and grab the washing up liquid – the worms will soon surface!

recycling bin

• Make a postbox from an old cardboard box. Cut a slot to post your letters through, then write (or draw) some letters to post.
• Create your own bowling set using empty plastic bottles and a ball. This is a good indoor game for rainy or wintry afternoons!
• Make crazy masks from paper plates decorated with items found in your recycling box, such as paper, plastic lids and baking foil.

bathtime

• Make fun and foamy bathpaints by mixing up shaving foam and food colouring in plastic beakers.
• Have fun pouring and squirting water from old shampoo, soap or handwash bottles.
• Try a sink/float experiment: gather a selection of household objects together, then have fun guessing which ones will sink and which will float!
• Play with ice cubes in the bath.

role play

• Do the washing. Make a child-sized washing line with some string and a couple of sticks stuck in the ground. Then have some fun 'washing' clothes and pegging them on the line.
• If you have a large cardboard box, put it on its side and open a shop or café. Stock it with bits and pieces from around the house.
• If your little one is into transport, line up all your kitchen chairs – they make great buses and trains.

miscellaneous

• On a rainy day, get out a pile of blankets, bedcovers and sheets and drape them over chairs and tables to make a hideaway or den.
• Make some homemade bubble mixture and bend pipe cleaners/chenille stems into wands, then get blowing!
• Sit around the kitchen table and make straw necklaces.

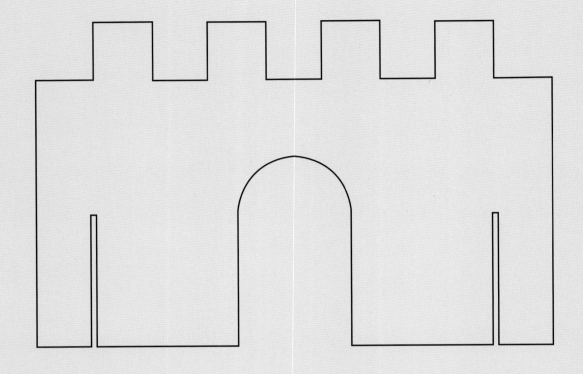

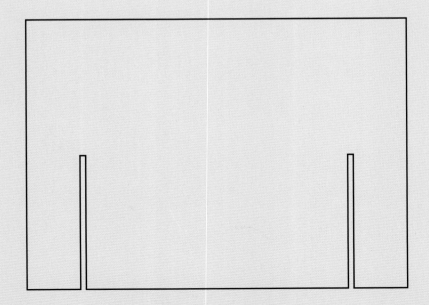

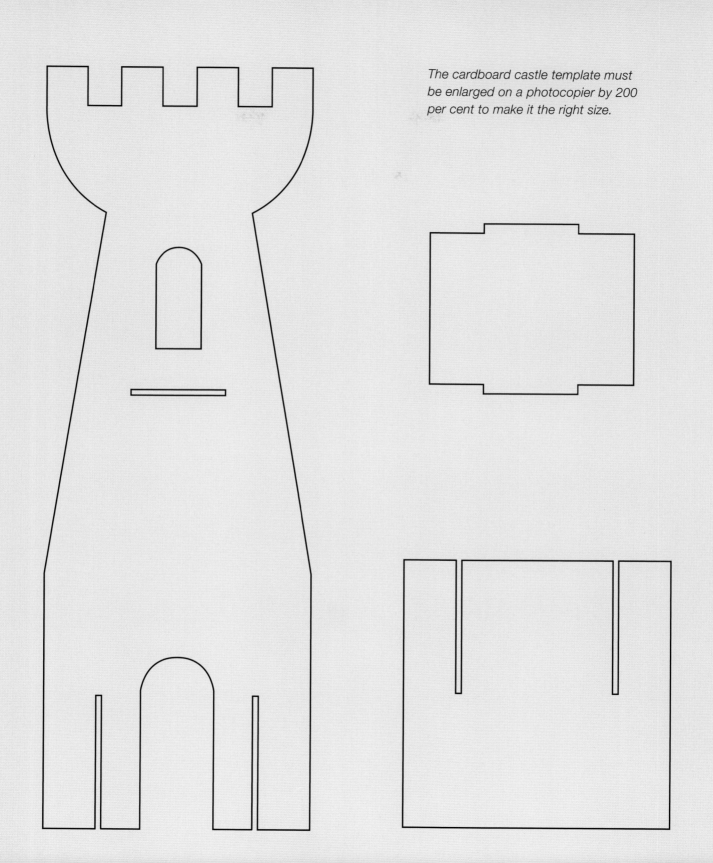

The cardboard castle template must be enlarged on a photocopier by 200 per cent to make it the right size.

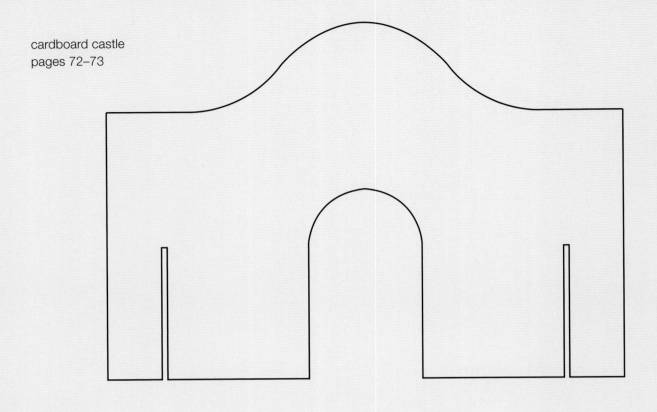

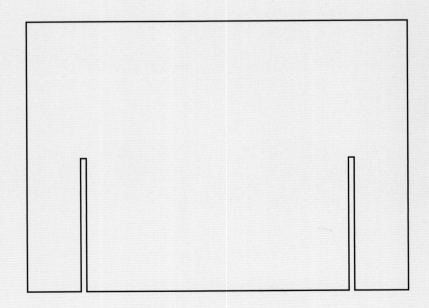

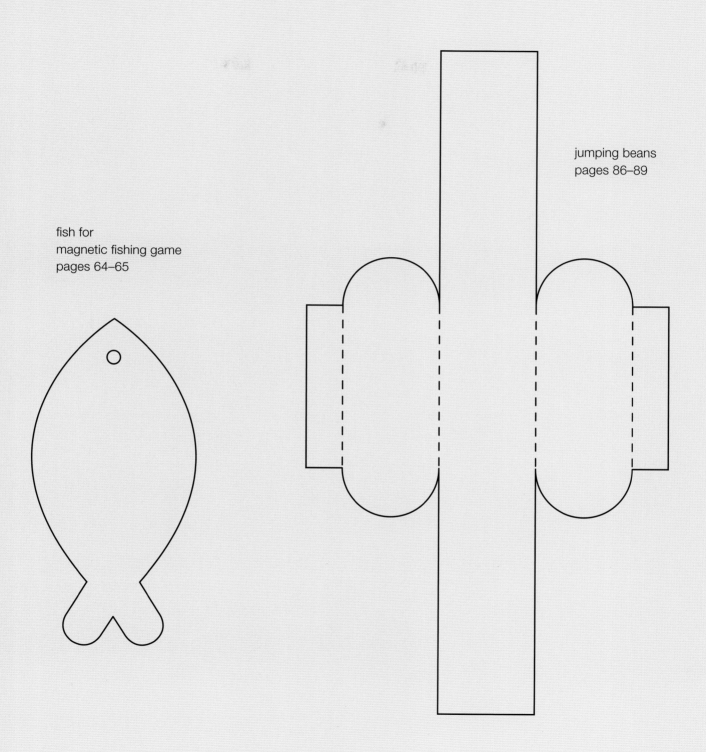

fish for
magnetic fishing game
pages 64–65

jumping beans
pages 86–89

shadow makers
pages 76–77

Pac-man mobile
Pages 84–85

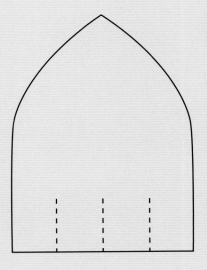

sock hobby horse ear
pages 96–99

sewing cards
pages 102–103

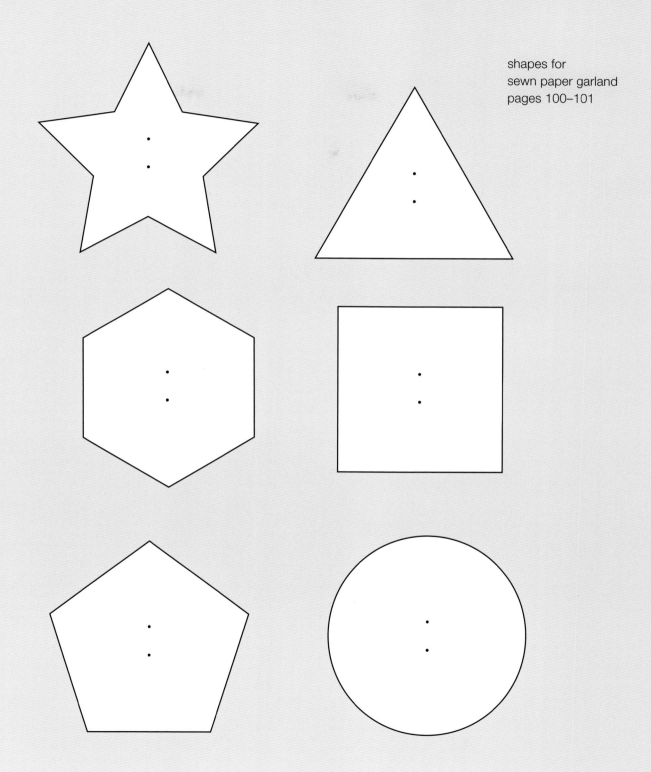

shapes for
sewn paper garland
pages 100–101

directory of suppliers

Superstores

Hobbycraft
http://www.hobbycraft.co.uk
Chain of UK crafting superstores that will meet all your crafting needs. Either check out the store locator on the website to find your nearest store or shop online.

Michaels
http://www.michaels.com
A chain of North American crafting stores that will meet all your crafting needs. Either check out the store locator on the website to find your nearest store or shop online.

Paperchase
http://www.paperchase.co.uk
Nationwide UK chain that's great for coloured paper, metallic gel pens, card and ribbon as well as unusual gifts and cute stationery. Check out the store locator on the website to find your nearest store or shop online.

Screwfix (UK)
http://www.screwfix.com
Great for nuts, bolts and any other tools and fixings you may need for the projects in this book. Check out the store locator on the website to find your nearest store or shop online.

Spotlight
http://www.spotlight.com.au
Australian website and chain of craft stores. Fantastic for all things crafty. Check out the website to order a catalogue and find your nearest store or shop online.

Smaller retailers

The Bargain Home Shop
http://stores.ebay.co.uk/The -Bargain-Home-Shop
Untreated wooden curtain rings for the Ribbon Rings project on pages 38–39.

Beadingcrafty
www.beadingcrafty.com
Great for beads, charms and jewellery findings.

Cakes, Cookies and Crafts
www.cakescookiesandcrafts shop.co.uk
Large selection of different food colourings and tints in every imaginable shade. Also cookie cutters for the Easy Birdfeeder on pages 50–51.

Guy's Magnets
http://stores.ebay.co.uk/Guy s-Magnets
Supplier of neodymium magnets for the Magnetic Fishing Game on pages 64–65.

Jaswallhead
http://stores.ebay.co.uk/jasw allhead
Supplier of threading laces and other craft supplies.

Jodie's Stencils and Punches
http://stores.ebay.co.uk/jodi esstencilsandpunches
Supplier of craft punches.

Little Crafty Bugs
www.littlecraftybugs.co.uk
Good selection of kids' craft punches and colourful card and googly eyes.

Maxumtradecraft
http://stores.ebay.co.uk/max umtradecraft
Great for bells, beads, charms and findings.

Patteson's Glass
http://www.jarsandbottles.co .uk/
Small glass bottles and jars for the Jar of Love project on pages 78–79.

Purpleroomcrafts
http://stores.ebay.co.uk/pur pleroomcrafts/
Suppliers of mirror card and other crafty supplies.

Shipwreck Beads
www.shipwreckbeads.com
Large selection of plastic beads in every colour and shape imaginable. Good for the Kaleidescope project on pages 54–55.

Blogs and websites

Chez Beeper Bebe
http://www.chezbeeperbebe.
blogspot.com/
*Crafty blogger with an Etsy
shop.*

How About Orange
http://www.howaboutorange
.blogspot.com/
A blog that's brimming with
craft tutorials, DIY projects,
free downloads, decorating
tips, and design inspiration
for adults.

Say YES! to Hoboken
http://www.sayyestohoboken
.com/
*Inspiring blog all about
stylish and crafty living.
Aimed at adults, but includes
some kids' crafting projects.*

Poppytalk
http://www.poppytalk.blogsp
ot.com/p/about-us.html
*Poppytalk is a Canadian
design blog dedicated
to promoting emerging
design talent. Gorgeous
projects and printables.*

Whipup
http://www.whipup.net
*Whip Up was founded in
2006 by Kathreen Ricketson.
Its aim is to bring the best
original and exciting crafts to
the attention of many. Worth
visiting for the cute tutorials
from guest bloggers.*

Ikat bag
http://www.ikatbag.com
*Cute, colourful blog that
focusses on sewing and
cardboard crafts.*

Meet me at Mikes
http://www.meetmeatmikes.
com/
*If you want to learn to
crochet, this is the place to
visit. Great for recipes and
general chit-chat!*

Red Ted Art's blog
http://www.redtedart.com/
*Hundreds of fun ideas for
crafting with kids.*

Oh Happy Day!
http://www.ohhappyday.com/
*Gorgeous and inspiring
design blog aimed at adults.*

What I Made
http://www.whatimade.com/
*A quirky arts and crafts blog
containing an eclectic mix of
do-it-yourself craft projects
all accompanied by fun hand
drawn tutorials.*

The Journals of Giddy Giddy
http://blog.giddygiddy.com/
*Inspiring blog of designer
and crafter Teri Dimalanta.
Features experiments with
felt, paint and textiles.*

Made by Joel
http://www.madebyjoel.com/
*Made by Joel is a space to
share art, craft, and
handmade education
projects for children and their
care givers.*

Tinkerlab
http://www.tinkerlab.com
*Rachelle Doorley's blog
contains hundreds of
creative experiments for you
to try out with your kids.*

Arvindgupta Toys
http://www.arvindguptatoys.
com/toys.html
*A wonderful website with lots
of fascinating experiments
and heaps of tutorials on
making toys from trash.*

E-coloriage
www.e-coloriage.com
*French website with free
cute and quirky colouring
pages for kids, all with an
environmental theme.*

Curly Birds
http://www.curlybirds.typepa
d.com/
*Curly Birds is a blog devoted
to crafts for children and the
art of play. Lots of whimsical
ideas for crafting and
decorations and particularly
good for cute sewing
projects for preschoolers.*

index

acknowledgements

I would like to say a huge thank you to Carolyn Barber for all her wonderful photography. Thanks also to Sonya Nathoo and Annabel Morgan for their general support and for all the super work they have done on the design, layout and text.

Thank you to all the gorgeous kids who modelled for the book and played with all the projects so enthusiastically.

And, finally, thank you to Seth and Tom, for inspiring me, and for making me a really happy Mum!

Ryland, Peters and Small would like to thank all the children who modelled for this book, including Giselle, Hope, Jack, Lola, Lucas, Mia, Rosie, Ruby, Sammy and Zak.